Happy Cooking Mirusona

With lots of love & famous

Thammy

June 2010

Pune.

Cooking with KIDS

TARLA DALAL

SANJAY & CO.
BOMBAY

Fourth Edition 2009

"Tarla Dalal" is also a registered trademark owned by Sanjay & Co.

Copyright © Sanjay & Company

ISBN: 978-8-186469-47-7

Price : Rs. **189/-**

Published & Distributed by :
SANJAY & COMPANY
353/A-1, Shah & Nahar Industrial Estate, Dhanraj Mill Compound, Lower Parel (W), Mumbai - 400 013. INDIA.
Tel. : (91-22) 4345 2400 • Fax : (91-22) 2496 5876 • E-mail : sanjay@tarladalal.com • E-mail : www.tarladalal.com

For book purchase enquiry & tarladalal.com membership, call our Toll Free Number : 1 800 209 3252 from any landline or mobile in India.

UK and USA customers can call us on :
UK : 02080029533 ● USA : 213-634-1406
For books, Membership on **tarladalal.com**, Subscription for **Cooking & More** and Recipe queries
Timing : 9.30 a.m. to 7.00 p.m. (IST), from Monday to Saturday
Local call charges applicable

Research Team	Designed by	Food Stylist	Photography	Production Designer	Printed by :
Pinky Dixit	S. Kishor	Nitin Tandon	Vinay Mahidhar	Maria D'souza	Minal Sales Agencies, Mumbai.
Arati Fedane					
Prasad Lele					

COOK BOOKS BY TARLA DALAL

INDIAN COOKING
Tava Cooking
Rotis & Subzis
Desi Khana
The Complete Gujarati Cook Book
Mithai
Chaat
Achaar aur Parathe
The Rajasthani Cookbook
Swadisht Subzian
Punjabi Khana New
Mughlai Khana New
South Indian Recipes New

TOTAL HEALTH
Low Calorie Healthy Cooking
Pregnancy Cookbook
Baby and Toddler Cookbook
Cooking with 1 Teaspoon of Oil
Home Remedies
Delicious Diabetic Recipes
Fast Foods Made Healthy
Healthy Soups & Salads
Healthy Breakfast
Calcium Rich Recipes
Healthy Heart Cook Book
Forever Young Diet
Healthy Snacks
Iron Rich Recipes
Healthy Juices
Low Cholesterol Recipes
Good Food for Diabetes

WESTERN COOKING
The Complete Italian Cookbook
The Chocolate Cookbook
Eggless Desserts
Mocktails & Snacks
Thai Cooking
Soups & Salads
Mexican Cooking
Chinese Cooking
Easy Chinese Cooking
Sizzlers & Barbeques
Cakes & Pastries New
Party Drinks New
Wraps & Rolls New

Healthy Subzis
Healthy Snacks for Kids
High Blood Pressure Cook Book
Low Calorie Sweets
Nutritious Recipes for Pregnancy
Diabetic Snacks
Zero Oil Rotis & Subzis
Zero Oil Soups, Salads & Snacks
Zero Oil Dal & Chawal
Acidity Cook Book
Growing Kids Cookbook
Soya Rotis & Subzis
Cooking with Sprouts
Exotic Diabetic Cooking - Part 1 New
Healthy Diabetic Cooking New
Protein Rich Recipes New
Eat Well Stay Well New

MINI SERIES
Cooking Under 10 minutes
Pizzas and Pasta
Fun Food for Children
Roz ka Khana
Idlis & Dosas
Microwave - Desi Khana
Paneer
Parathas
Chawal
Dals
Sandwiches
Quick Cooking
Curries & Kadhis
Chinese Recipes
Jain Desi Khana
7 Dinner Menus
Jain International Recipes

Punjabi Subzis
Chips & dips
Corn
Microwave Subzis
Baked Dishes
Stir-Fry
Potatoes
Recipes Using Leftovers
Noodles
Lebenese
Cook Book for Two's
Know your Dals & Pulses
Fruit & Vegetable Carving
Know your Spices
Know your Flours
Popular Restaurant Gravies New
Paneer Snacks New
Know Your Green Leafy Vegetables New

GENERAL COOKING
Exciting Vegetarian Cooking
Microwave Recipes
Saatvik Khana
The Pleasures of Vegetarian Cooking
The Delights of Vegetarian Cooking
The Joys of Vegetarian Cooking
Cooking with Kids
Snacks Under 10 Minutes
Ice-Cream & Frozen Desserts
Desserts Under 10 Minutes
Entertaining
Microwave Snacks & Desserts
Kebabs & Tikkis New
Non-fried Snacks New

This book is dedicated to

all children and

in particular to my

granddaughters

Mitali and Tarini

Tarla Dalal

INDEX

SANDWICHES

CAKES AND BAKES

DESSERTS

BEFORE YOU START

GOLDEN RULE:
Look out for

It means that the step is difficult. So, ask an adult to help you.

TIPS FOR COOKING

1. Always ask an adult for permission before you enter the kitchen.
2. Always read the whole recipe before you start cooking.
3. Measure all the ingredients correctly before you start cooking.
4. When chopping or cutting vegetables, be sure to use a chopping board.
5. Always turn the sharp edge of knife away from you when you chop.
6. To test food, always use a spoon or fork. Never put your finger into the food.

TIPS FOR BAKING

1. Always ask an adult to preheat the oven.
2. While using oven or toaster, always wear rubber slippers. Never touch electrical switches.
3. Never switch on the oven with wet hands.
4. Always wear oven gloves to remove anything from the oven.
5. Do not open the oven door while food is baking.

Number of thumbs indicates the level of difficulty.

👍 Easy   👍👍 A little care needed   👍👍👍 More care needed

FIRST AID

FOR BURNS

1. Cool the burnt parts under cold water for at least 10 minutes.
2. Ask an adult to help you to apply burn ointment. Keep the burn covered so that it does not get infected.
3. If someone's clothing catches fire, do not panic. Try and remove the clothing or pour lots of cold water over the person to stop the burning.

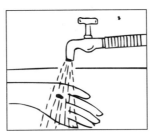

FOR CUTS

1. Wash the cut with antiseptic solution.
2. Cover with cotton wool to stop the bleeding.
3. Apply antiseptic cream or used a medicated Band-Aid, so that it does not get infected.
4. If the cut does not stop bleeding for a while, you might need an adult to help you or call a doctor.

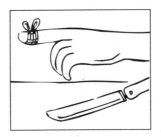

EQUIPMENTS

For Preparation

Small knife

Vegetable peeler

Spatula

Large knife

Apple corer

Scraper

Can opener

Pizza cutter

Pastry brush

Ice cream scoop

Juicer

Blender

Whisk

Mixing bowl

Chopping board

Masher

Sieve

Colander

Grater

For Measuring

Teaspoon ($\frac{1}{4}$, $\frac{1}{2}$, 1)   Tablespoon (1)   Cups ($\frac{1}{4}$, $\frac{1}{3}$, $\frac{1}{2}$, 1)   Glass

For Baking

Setting Tray   Muttin moulds   Rolling pin

Baking Tray   Small tart moulds   Cookie cutters   Paper cups

For Cooking

Saucepans with lids   Frying pan   Toaster

Flat spoon   Wooden spoon

For Serving

Serving bowl   Serving plate   Spoons   Soup Bowl

Forks

9

FOR YOUR KNOWLEDGE

Beast : To mix and soften the mixture using a wooden spoon, wire whisk, egg beater or electric mixer.

Boil : To heat the liquid till bubbles rise on the surface and break. Steam also starts to rise.

Chop : To cut into small pieces using a knife.

Crush : To break into smaller pieces using a rolling pin.

Drain : To strain away unwanted liquid by using a strainer. Do this over a kitchen sink.

Deep frying : To cook food in very hot oil, butter, vanaspati, ghee in a deep vessel or kadai.

Shallow frying : To cook food in a shallow pan / tava / non-stick pan using very little oil.

Garnish : To decorate.

Grease : To spread butter or vanaspati on the bottom and sides of a dish using a pastry brush, or by hand.

Peel : To remove the skin using a peeler.

Pinch : Quantity that you can pick between your thumb and forefinger.

Preheat : To heat the oven to a set temperature according to the recipe before you start cooking. But remember, ask an adult to do this.

Prick : To make holes using a fork.

Simmer : To heat the liquid till the bubbles start rising, keeping it on a low flame.

Slice : To cut a thin, flat piece from a larger piece.

Soak : To dip in water or any other liquid to make it soft.

Stir : To mix with a spoon.

Strain : To pass through a sieve.

Toast : To brown the bread or any other food article in an oven or a toaster.

Whisk : To mix using a wire whisk to remove lumps and make a smooth batter or mixture.

DRINKS

STRAWBERRY BANANA MILKSHAKE

Makes 4 glasses.

What you will need
2 glasses cold milk
1 cup strawberries or
4 tablespoons strawberry crush
2 bananas
2 to 4 tablespoons sugar
4 ice cubes

Equipment needed
knife
blender
chopping board
tablespoons
4 glasses
4 straws

1. Wash the strawberries. Remove the stems & cut into half.

2. Peel the bananas. Chop into 4 to 5 pieces each.

3. Pour milk into the blender, add strawberries, bananas, sugar & ice cubes.

4. Put the lid on the blender & blend well until smooth.

5. Pour into 4 glasses.

6. Pop in straws.

Serve immediately.

💡 If you use strawberry crush, use less sugar.
💡 Ice cubes make noise, don't get scared.

ROSE FALOODA

Makes 4 glasses.

What you will need
2 tablespoons sabza (takhmariya)
3 glasses cold milk
6 teaspoons rose syrup
4 ice cubes
4 scoops vanilla ice-cream

Equipment needed
teaspoons
tablespoons
bowl
ice-cream scoop
4 glasses

1. Soak the sabza in 1 glass of water for 10 minutes.

2. Drain all the excess water out of the sabza.

3. Divide the soaked sabza equally into 4 glasses.

4. In a bowl, mix the cold milk, ice cubes & rose syrup.

5. Pour into the glasses over the sabza.

6. Top each with a scoop of vanilla ice-cream.

Serve immediately.

You can use Kesar Syrup instead of Rose Syrup and hey!
You have KESAR FALOODA.

SODA FOUNTAIN

Makes 1 glasses.

What you will need
2 tablespoons of your
  favourite fruit syrup
1 scoop vanilla ice-cream
1 bottle (200 ml.) soda, chilled

Equipment needed
tablespoons
bottle opener
ice-cream scoop
1 tall glass

13

1. Pour the syrup into a glass and add the vanilla ice-cream. Stir slightly.

2. Open the bottle of soda & pour over the ice-cream.

Serve immediately.
You can also make a cola float with vanilla ice-cream and your favourite cola.

STRAWBERRY FLIP

Makes 1 tall glass. *Picture on page 53*

What you will need	**To garnish**	**Equipment needed**
2 tablespoons fresh chopped strawberries	1 cherry	ice-cream scoop
	mint leaves	tablespoons
1 scoop vanilla ice-cream		cup
½ cup cold milk		blender
1 tablespoon sugar		1 tall glass
4 ice cubes		

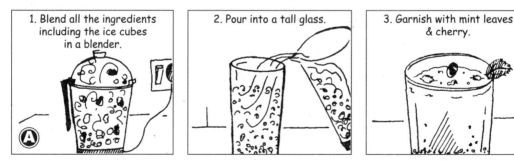

1. Blend all the ingredients including the ice cubes in a blender.

2. Pour into a tall glass.

3. Garnish with mint leaves & cherry.

Serve immediately.
You can also use chickoo, banana, apple or mango.

ICED EXPRESSO

Makes 4 glasses. *Picture on page 35*

What you will need
3   cups chilled milk
4   ice cubes
4   tablespoons sugar
½ teaspoon cinnamon powder
1   teaspoon cocoa powder
1½ teaspoons coffee powder
½ teaspoon vanilla essence
4   scoops of vanilla or
    chocolate ice-cream

Equipment needed
cups
blender
tablespoon
teaspoons
4 glasses

1. Put chilled milk & ice cubes into a blender.

2. Add the sugar, cinnamon powder, cocoa powder, coffee powder & vanilla essence. Blend till frothy.

3. Place one scoop of ice-cream in each glass.

4. Pour the blended coffee over the ice-cream. Pop a teaspoon in each glass.

Serve immediately.
Iced Expresso tastes wonderful without the ice-cream, too.

FRUITY ICED TEA

Makes 4 glasses. *Picture on page 17*

What you will need
1 glass orange juice
2 tea bags
2 glasses water
4 tablespoons sugar
16 ice cubes

To garnish
mint leaves
4 orange slices

Equipment needed
saucepan
knife
chopping board
tablespoons
4 tall glasses

1. Put 1 glass of water, the sugar & tea bags in a saucepan & bring to boil.

2. Cool & remove the tea bags.

3. When the tea is completely cold, add the orange juice & 1 more glass of water.

4. Put 4 ice cubes in each glass and pour the tea mixture over it.

5. Garnish with a slice of orange & mint leaves.

Serve immediately.

You can also use apple juice or pineapple juice instead of the orange juice.

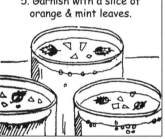

1. Walnut Raisin Truffles, *page 73.*
2. Fruity Iced Tea, *page 16.*
3. Jelly Boats, *page 75*
4. Aloo Chaat, *page 30.*

16

CHOCO-MALLOW

Makes 4 cups.

What you will need
3   cups milk
1   cup water
4   teaspoons cocoa powder
4   teaspoons sugar
4   white marshmallows

Equipment needed
saucepan
teaspoons
4 cups

1. In a saucepan, combine the milk, water, cocoa powder & sugar.

2. Stir well to break any lumps & bring to a boil. Ⓐ

3. Place 1 marshmallow in each cup.

4. Pour the hot liquid over the marshmallows. Ⓐ

Serve immediately.

💡 Choco Mallow tastes good even without the marshmallows. Just sprinkle some grated chocolate top.

1.   Macaroni and Vegetable Salad, *page 25.*
2.   Potato Salad, *page 26.*
3.   Chana Chaat, *page 31*
4.   Chat-pati Frankies, *page 32.*

CINDERELLA

Makes 1 glass. *Picture on page 35*

What you will need

3   teaspoons raspberry syrup
1   teaspoon lemon juice
3   tablespoons fruits, finely chopped
    (pineapple, pears, apple)
1   bottle lemonade or any lemon drink

Equipment needed

tablespoons
teaspoons
bottle opener
knife
chopping board
1 tall glass

1. Put the raspberry syrup & lemon juice in a tall serving glass.

2. Add the fruits.

3. Open the bottle of lemonade & pour it into the glass.

Serve chilled.

You can also use strawberry crush instead of raspberry syrup.

SOUPS AND SALADS

SWEET CORN SOUP

Serves 4.

What you will need
1 can cream style corn (450 grams)
1 tablespoon cornflour
3½ cups water
1 tablespoon butter
salt and pepper to taste

Equipment needed
can opener
tablespoons
knife
cups
saucepan
4 soup bowls

1. Open a can of corn.

2. Add the cornflour to ½ cup of water & mix into a paste. Keep aside.

3. Heat the butter in a saucepan.

4. Add the corn & 3 cups of water and mix well.

5. Add the cornflour & water mixture & bring to a boil.

6. Let it boil for 2 to 3 minutes & add salt & pepper.

7. Pour into soup bowls.

Serve hot.

You can serve with hot Cheese Garlic Buns, recipe on page 55.

QUICK VEGETABLE SOUP

Serves 4. *Picture on page 54*

What you will need

2   spring onions
6   spinach leaves
1   carrot
1   cup milk
2   cups water
3   teaspoons cornflour
2   to 3 tablespoons grated cheese
salt and peeper to taste

Equipment needed

knife
chopping board
peeler
grater
cups
saucepan
teaspoons
tablespoons
4 soup bowls

1. Chop the spring onions & cut the spinach leaves.

2. Peel & grate the carrot.

3. Pour the milk, water & cornflour into a saucepan & mix well.

4. Add the spring onions, spinach & carrot and bring to a boil.

5. Add the cheese, salt & pepper. Mix well.

6. Pour into 4 soup bowls.

Serve hot.

Be sure to wash the vegetables properly before cutting them.

VEGETABLE NOODLE SOUP

Serves 4.

What you will need
2   carrots
1   tomato
½   cup cabbage
2   spring onions
1   capsicum
1   tablespoon oil
½   packet 2 minute noodles
4   cups water
1   tablespoon cornflour
salt and pepper to taste

Equipment needed
peeler
grater
knife
chopping board
cups
saucepan
tablespoons
4 soup bowls

1. Peel & grate the carrots.

2. Chop the tomato, spring onions & cabbage into small pieces.

3. Cut the capsicum into halves. Remove the seeds & cut into thin slices.

4. Heat the oil in a saucepan, add all the vegetables & stir for a few minutes.

5. Add 4 cups of water & the noodles to the vegetables & bring to a boil.

6. Mix the cornflour in a little water & add to the soup.

7. Add salt & pepper. Mix well & pour into soup bowls.

Serve hot.
Serve this soup with soya sauce.

MACARONI AND VEGETABLE SALAD

Serves 4. *Picture on page 18*

What you will need
2 cups boiled macaroni
2 spring onions
1 capsicum
1 tomato
½ cup cheese
½ cup sweet corn kernels
¼ cup boiled peas
2 tablespoons lemon juice
1 teaspoon sugar
salt & peeper to taste

Equipment needed
knife
chopping board
mixing bowl
cups
teaspoons
tablespoons
1 serving plate

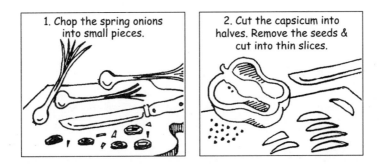

1. Chop the spring onions into small pieces.

2. Cut the capsicum into halves. Remove the seeds & cut into thin slices.

3. Cut the tomato & cheese into small cubes.

4. In a mixing bowl, mix together all the vegetables, macaroni & cheese cubes.

5. Add the lemon juice, sugar, salt & peeper. Mix well & refrigerate.

Serve chilled.
Remember to use cooled macaroni for your salad.

POTATO SALAD

Serves 4. *Picture on page 18*

What you will need	**Equipment needed**
4 boiled potatoes	knife
1 capsicum	chopping board
1 cup lettuce	toaster
2 cheese cubes	cups
4 bread slices	tablespoons
3 tablespoons mayonnaise	1 small mixing bowl
1 tablespoon milk	1 large serving bowl
1 tablespoon tomato ketchup	

1. Peel & cut the potatoes into cubes.

2. Wash & cut the capsicum into halves. Remove the seeds & cut into medium sized pieces.

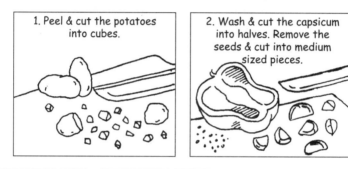

3. Wash & tear the lettuce by hand into small pieces.

4. Cut the cheese cubes into small pieces.

5. Toast the bread slices till crisp. Cut each slice into cubes & keep aside.

6. In a small mixing bowl, mix together the mayonnaise, milk & tomato ketchup.

7. Put the potatoes, capsicum, lettuce, cheese & bread pieces into a large serving bowl.

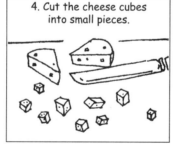

8. Add the mayonnaise mixture & mix well.

Serve immediately.

You can get eggless mayonnaise in the market.

SNACKS

NOUGHTS AND CROSSES PIZZA

Makes 1 pizza. *Picture on page 53*

What you will need

3   cheese slices
1   pizza base, 100 mm. (4")
    in diameter
pizza sauce (recipe on page 29)

6   capsicum strips
3   onion slices
3   tomato slices
butter to grease the tray

Equipment needed

knife
chopping board
oven
baking tray

1. Preheat the oven to 180°C (355°F).

2. Cut the cheese slices into thin strips.

3. Grease a baking tray with butter & place the pizza base on top.

4. Spread the pizza sauce on the base.

5. Arrange the cheese strips to form a criss-cross pattern on the pizza.

6. Place the tomato & onion slices alternately in between the cheese squares.

7. In the empty squares, make crosses with the capsicum strips.

8. Put the baking tray in the preheated oven & bake for 10 to 15 minutes.

Ⓐ **Remove from the oven & serve hot.**
💡 You can also make the pizza on bread slices.

PIZZA SAUCE

For 2 pizzas.

What you will need
4 tomatoes
1 onion
4 garlic flakes
1 teaspoon oregano
2 tablespoons butter
salt to taste

Equipment needed
teaspoon
tablespoon
knife
chopping board
saucepan

1. Boil water in a saucepan. Put the tomatoes in the boiling water for 1 minute. Remove & cool them.

2. Peel the tomatoes & chop them.

3. Peel & chop the onion & garlic.

4. Heat the butter in a saucepan. Add the onion & garlic. Fry till they are brown.

5. Add the tomatoes & cook for 7-10 minutes.

6. Add the oregano & salt.

If you do not have time to make pizza sauce, use 3 tablespoons of tomato ketchup and $\frac{1}{2}$ teaspoon of chilli sauce instead.

ALOO CHAAT

Serve 4. *Picture on page 17*

What you will need
16 boiled baby
   potatoes, peeled
1 small onion
1 tomato
1 capsicum
1 tablespoon lemon juice
½ teaspoon sugar
1½ teaspoons chaat masala
1 tablespoon chopped
   coriander leaves

Equipment needed
knife
chopping board
peeler
mixing bowl
teaspoons
tablespoons
1 serving bowl

1. Peel the onion & cut into small pieces

2. Cut the tomato into cubes.

3. Cut the capsicum into half. Remove the seeds & cut into small pieces

4. Mix the potatoes, onion, tomatoes & capsicum in a mixing bowl.

5. Add the lemon juice, sugar & chaat masala & mix well.

6. Put the aloo chaat in a serving bowl and sprinkle coriander leaves on top.

Serve chilled.
You can also add date/tamarind chutney, if you like.

CHANA CHAAT

Serve 4. *Picture on page 18*

What you will need

1½ cups boiled chick peas (Kabuli chana)
½ cup paneer
1 cucumber
1 spring onion

2 tablespoons tomato ketchup
1 teaspoon chaat masala
1 tablespoon chopped coriander leaves

Equipment needed

knife
chopping board
peeler
cup
teaspoons
tablespoons
mixing bowl
1 serving bowl

1. Cut the paneer into small cubes.

2. Peel the cucumber & cut into small pieces.

3. Chop the spring onion.

4. Put the chick peas, paneer, cucumber & spring onion in a mixing bowl.

5. Add the tomato ketchup & chaat masala & mix well.

6. Put in a serving bowl & sprinkle the coriander leaves on top.

Refrigerate. Serve chilled.

You can also add mint chutney instead of chaat masala and make your **Hara Bhara Chane Ka Chaat.**

CHAT - PATI FRANKIES

Makes 4 frankies. *Picture on page 18*

What you will need
4 chapaties
2 boiled potatoes
½ cup grated paneer
1 carrot, peeled and grated
1 cheese cube, grated

2 teaspoons chaat masala
1 tablespoon lemon juice
1 tomato, cut into strips
1 capsicum, cut into strips
salt to taste

Equipment needed
knife
peeler
grater
mixing bowl
chopping board
teaspoons
tablespoons
serving plates

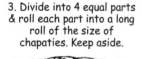

1. Peel & grate the boiled potatoes & place in a mixing bowl.

2. Add the paneer, carrot, cheese, half the chaat masala, the lemon juice & salt & mix well.

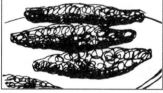

3. Divide into 4 equal parts & roll each part into a long roll of the size of chapaties. Keep aside.

4. Warm the chapaties & place on a serving plate.

5. Put one roll of the potato & paneer mixture in the centre of a chapati.

6. Put some capsicum & tomato strips & sprinkle some chaat masala on top.

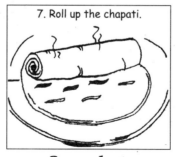

7. Roll up the chapati.

8. Repeat with the other chapaties.

Serve hot.

Ask mummy to make some extra chapaties when she is making them for lunch or dinner.

CHEESY POTATO BAKE

Serves 4.

What you will need
4   potatoes
2   onions
½ cup grated cheese
½ teaspoon pepper powder
½ cup milk
butter to grease the baking dish

Equipment needed
peeler
knife
chopping board
grater
cups
teaspoon
oven
baking dish

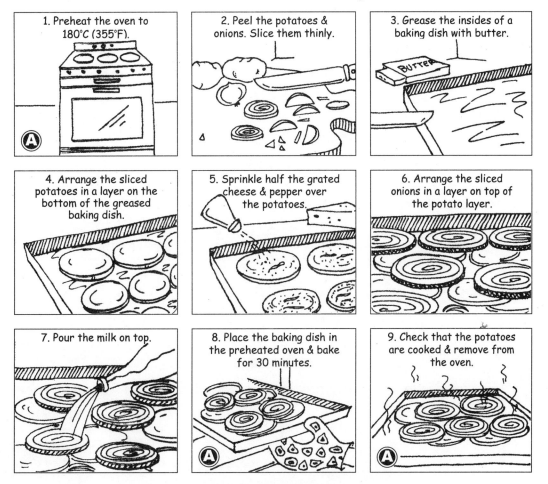

1. Preheat the oven to 180°C (355°F).

2. Peel the potatoes & onions. Slice them thinly.

3. Grease the insides of a baking dish with butter.

4. Arrange the sliced potatoes in a layer on the bottom of the greased baking dish.

5. Sprinkle half the grated cheese & pepper over the potatoes.

6. Arrange the sliced onions in a layer on top of the potato layer.

7. Pour the milk on top.

8. Place the baking dish in the preheated oven & bake for 30 minutes.

9. Check that the potatoes are cooked & remove from the oven.

Serve hot with garlic bread.

💡 You can reduce on the cooking time by using half-boiled potatoes.

ALOO TIKKIS

Makes 8 tikkis. *Picture on page 35*

What you will need
4 boiled potatoes, peeled
½ cup boiled green peas
1 tablespoon chopped
    coriander leaves
½ teaspoon chilli powder
1 teaspoon chaat masala
juice of ½ lemon
salt to taste
2 tablespoons oil to fry
    the tikkis

Equipment needed
masher
peeler
cups
teaspoon
tablespoons
cookie cutter
frying pan
flat spoon
mixing bowl
1 serving plate

1. Put the potatoes & peas in a mixing bowl & mash well till no lumps remain.

2. Add the coriander leaves, chilli powder, chaat masala, lemon juice & salt and mix well.

3. Divide into 8 portions & roll into round patties.

4. Cut out shapes using a cookie cutter.

5. Heat the oil, in a frying pan & shallow fry all the tikkis on both sides till golden brown.

6. Put in a serving plate & serve hot with ketchup.

You can grate the potatoes if you find it difficult to mash them.

1. Banana Walnut Muffins, *page 58*.
2. Jam Tarts, *page 61*.
3. Iced Expresso, *page 15*.
4. Cinderella, *page 20*.
5. Bean and Cheese Burgers, *page 49*.
6. Chilli-Cheese Toast, *page 51*.
7. Aloo Tikkis, *page 34*.

SUMMER TACOS

Makes 6 tacos. *Picture on page 36*

What you will need
6   taco shells
1   small can (225 grams) baked beans
½ cup grated carrots
½ cup shredded cabbage
1   tablespoon chopped coriander leaves
½ teaspoon sugar
1   teaspoon lemon juice
½ cup grated cheese
2   tablespoons green chilli sauce
salt to taste

Equipment needed
can opener
grater
knife
chopping board
cups
teaspoons
tablespoons
mixing bowl
1 serving dish

1. Open the can of baked beans.

2. In a mixing bowl, mix the carrots, cabbage, coriander, sugar, lemon juice and salt.

3. In each taco shell, put about 2 tablespoons of baked beans.

4. Put some of the carrot & cabbage mixture on top of the baked beans.

5. Sprinkle some cheese on top and pour some of the green chilli sauce on top.

6. Repeat with the remaining taco shells and ingredients.

Serve immediately.
You can use small crisp puries instead of taco shells.

1. Flapjacks, *page 68.*
2. Tricolour Sandwiches, *page 50.*
3. Summer Tacos, *page 37.*

CHE-MATO PASTA

Serves 3 to 4. *Picture on page 54*

What you will need
2   cups boiled macaroni
1   onion
1   clove garlic
1   capsicum
½   cup tomato purée
½   cup tomato ketchup

3   tablespoons milk
½   cup grated cheese
1   tablespoon butter
salt and peeper to taste
some grated cheese for topping

Equipment needed
peeler
grater
knife
chopping board
cups
tablespoons
saucepan
1 serving plate

1. Peel & chop the onion.

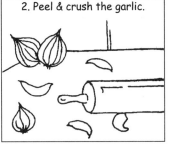

2. Peel & crush the garlic.

3. Cut the capsicum into half. Remove the seeds & cut into thin strips.

4. Heat the butter in a saucepan.

5. Add the onion & garlic and fry for a few minutes.

6. Add the capsicum, tomato purée & ketchup & stir for five minutes.

7. Add the milk, cheese, salt and pepper & mix well.

8. Add the boiled macaroni & mix well.

9. Put in a serving plate & sprinkle some grated cheese on top.

Serve hot.
This is an ideal, easy-to-make one-dish meal.

QUICK DAHI VADA

Serves 4.

What you will need
4 large butter biscuits
2 cups fresh curds
1 teaspoon cumin powder
a pinch chilli powder
1 tablespoon chopped
    coriander leaves
salt to taste

Equipment needed
mixing bowl
cups
teaspoon
tablespoon
knife
chopping board
whisk
saucepan
1 serving plate

1. Heat 2 cups of water in a saucepan.

2. Soak the butter biscuits in hot water for 5 to 7 minutes, turning on both sides.

3. Squeeze out water from the butter biscuits & place in a serving plate.

4. In a mixing bowl, mix the curds & salt & beat well with a whisk.

5. Pour the beaten curds on top of the butter biscuits.

6. Sprinkle the cumin & chilli powder on top.

7. Garnish with chopped coriander leaves.

Serve chilled.
Do not soak the butter biscuits for long as they will break.

BAKED POTATOES

Serves 4. *Picture on page 54*

What you will need
4 medium potatoes, boiled
½ cup grated cheese
3 tablespoons fresh cream
3 tablespoons butter
2 tablespoons boiled corn
2 tablespoons boiled green peas
1 tablespoon chopped
    coriander leaves

Equipment needed
baking dish
fork
mixing bowl
knife
chopping board
grater
tablespoons
cups
oven
4 ovenproof bowls or plates

1. Preheat the oven to 200°C (400°F)

2. Place one potato each in 4 ovenproof bowls.

3. Cut a cross in the centre of each potato. (Do not peel the potatoes.)

4. In a mixing bowl, mix together the cheese, cream, butter, corn, peas & coriander.

5. Put some of this mixture on top of each potato & bake for 10 minutes.

Ⓐ **Remove from the oven and serve hot.**

You can also top the potatoes with baked beans and cheese.

If you have a microwave oven, you can ask an adult to bake the potatoes with the skin in a few minutes & then proceed from step 3 onwards.

FRIED RICE

Serves 2.

What you will need
1   cup boiled rice
2   carrots
2   spring onions
½   capsicum
½   cup chopped cabbage
2   teaspoons soya sauce
4   tablespoons oil
salt to taste

Equipment needed
knife
chopping board
peeler
2 forks
cups
teaspoons
tablespoons
wok or frying pan

1. Wash, peel & chop the carrots into small pieces.

2. Wash & chop the spring onions into small pieces.

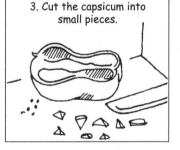

3. Cut the capsicum into small pieces.

4. Heat the oil in a wok.

5. Add all the vegetables & fry for a few minutes.

6. Add the soya sauce, rice & salt.

7. Mix well using 2 forks.

Serve hot.

You can grate the vegetables, if you do not want to cut them.

HAKKA NOODLES

Serves 2.

What you will need
1 cup boiled noodles
½ capsicum
2 spring onions
½ cup chopped cabbage
1 teaspoon chilli sauce
2 teaspoons soya sauce
4 teaspoons oil
salt to taste

Equipment needed
wok or frying pan
cups
teaspoons
knife
chopping board
2 forks

1. Wash & chop the spring onions into small pieces.

2. Cut the capsicum into small pieces.

3. Heat the oil in a wok.

4. Add the chopped cabbage, capsicum & spring onions.

5. Add the chilli sauce, soya sauce & noodles.

6. Add salt and mix well with 2 forks.

Serve hot.

You can put any vegetable that you like or even paneer in this dish.

CHEESE BOXES

Serves 4.

What you will need
1 small loaf sliced bread
1 small packet butter
1 cup grated cheese

Equipment needed
grater
cup
butter knife
baking tray
oven

1. Preheat the oven to 200°C (400°F)

2. Butter the bread slices on both sides using a butter knife.

3. Cut into small thin fingers.

4. Dip in grated cheese.

5. Put on a greased baking tray & bake for 20 to 25 minutes.

6. Remove the tray from the oven.

Serve hot.

Put a little chilli powder in the cheese to make **Chilli Cheese Boxes**.

CHEESY WAFERS

Serves 2.

What you will need
1 packet your favourite wafers
½ tablespoon grated cheese
½ teaspoon chilli powder

Equipment needed
grater
teaspoon
tablespoon
baking tray
oven
1 serving plate

1. Preheat the oven to 200°C (400°F)

2. In a baking tray, spread the wafers.

3. Sprinkle grated cheese & chilli powder on the wafers.

4. Bake for a few minutes till the cheese melts.

5. Serve hot on a serving plate.

💡 If you use spicy cheesy wafers, do not use chilli powder.
💡 You can also use nachos instead of wafers for **Cheesy Nachos.**

SANDWICHES

PIZZA SANDWICH

Makes 4 sandwiches.

What you will need

8 bread slices
butter
3 capsicums
2 tomatoes
1 onion

½ cup grated cheese
salt and pepper to taste

Equipment needed

knife
chopping board
cup
grater
mixing bowl
sandwich toaster

1. Switch on the sandwich toaster.

2. Apply butter on all the bread slices & keep aside.

3. Cut the capsicum into half, remove the seeds & cut into small pieces.

4. Wash & cut the tomatoes into small pieces.

5. Peel & chop the onion into small pieces.

6. Mix the onion, tomato & capsicum pieces in a mixing bowl.

7. Add the cheese, salt & pepper & mix well.

8. Place one slice of bread on the sandwich toaster & top with some of the filling mixture.

9. Place another slice of bread on top. Toast the sandwich for 4 to 5 minutes till golden brown.

(A) 10. Repeat for the remaining bread slices & filling mixture

Serve hot.

Apply butter on the outer side of the bread slices before putting the sandwich in the toaster.

CUCUMBER COTTAGE CHEESE SANDWICHES

Makes 4 sandwiches.

What you will need
8   bread slices
1   cucumber
1   cup grated paneer
1   tablespoon green chutney
salt to taste

Equipment needed
grater
peeler
knife
chopping board
cups
tablespoons
mixing bowl
1 serving plate

1. Peel the cucumber & grate it.

2. Sqeeze out the excess water from the cucumber.

3. Put the cucumber in a mixing bowl & add the paneer, butter, green chutney & salt.

4. Mix well till the mixture is smooth & creamy. Keep aside.

5. Spread a generous layer of this mixture on 4 slices of bread. Top with the remaining 4 slices.

6. Cut each sandwich into 4 pieces.

Serve with tomato ketchup.

💡 Sandwiches stay nice and fresh when wrapped in a damp cloth, plastic film or butter paper.

SUBMARINES

Makes 4 rolls. *Picture on page 64*

What you will need
4   hot dog rolls
1   carrot
1   beetroot
2   tablespoons lemon juice
butter
4   lettuce leaves
4   cheese slices
salt and peeper to taste

Equipment needed
peeler
grater
butter knife
knife
chopping board
tablespoons
mixing bowl
4 serving plates

1. Peel & grate the carrot & beetroot.

2. Put it into a mixing bowl. Add the salt, pepper & lemon juice. Mix well.

3. Cut each hot dog roll into half horizontally & place the lower half on to serving plates.

4. Spread some butter on each hot dog half. Top with a lettuce leaf & a slice of cheese.

5. Spread the carrot & beetroot mixture on top.

6. Cover with the other hot dog halves.

Cut the submarines, hold them together with toothpicks and then cut them.

BEAN AND CHEESE BURGERS

Makes 4 burgers. *Picture on page 35*

What you will need
4 bread buns
4 lettuce leaves
1 small can (225 grams) baked beans
4 cheese slices
½ teaspoon chilli flakes (paprika)

Equipment needed
can opener
knife
baking tray
teaspoon
oven
4 serving plates

1. Open the can of baked beans & then preheat the oven to 200°C (400°F).

2. Slice each bun horizontally into 2 halves & place them on a baking tray.

3. Bake for 5-7 minutes. Remove from the oven & transfer the bottom half on to serving plates.

4. Place the lettuce leaves on the bottom half of each bun and then spoon out baked beans on it.

5. Top with a slice of cheese & then sprinkle some paprika over it.

6. Cover each with the top half of the bun.

You can also use a can of Cream Style Corn instead of the baked beans.

49

TRICOLOR SANDWICHES

Makes 2 sandwiches. *Picture on page 36*

What you will need
6   bread slices
½   cup butter

For the green layer
½   cup grated paneer
2   tablespoons
     mint chutney
salt to taste

For the orange layer
½   cup grated carrots
2   tablespoons mayonnaise
salt to taste

Equipment needed
cups
tablespoons
butter knife
knife
grater
2 mixing bowl
1 serving plate

1. Butter the bread slices. Keep aside.

2. Mix the paneer, mint chutney & salt to a smooth paste in a mixing bowl to make the green layer.

3. Mix the grated carrots, mayonnaise & salt well in another mixing bowl to make the orange layer.

4. Spread the green layer on top of a bread slice.

5. Place another bread slice on top & spread the orange layer on it.

6. Put a third bread slice on top.

7. Cut into three strips.

8. Make another sandwich in the same way.

CHILLI-CHEESE TOAST

Makes 6 toasts. *Picture on page 35*

What you will need
6 bread slices
2 small capsicums
1 cup grated cheese
2 tablespoons tomato ketchup
2 tablespoons butter
½ teaspoon chilli sauce
For serving
tomato ketchup

Equipment needed
grater
knife
chopping board
mixing bowl
cup
teaspoons
tablespoons
oven
6 serving plates

1. Preheat the oven to 200°C (400°F)
Ⓐ

2. Cut each capsicum into half. Remove seeds & chop into small pieces.

3. In a mixing bowl, mix the cheese, tomato ketchup, butter, chilli sauce & capsicums.

4. Spread this mixture on the bread slices.

5. Place the bread slices on a baking tray.

6. Place the baking tray in the preheated oven & bake for 10 to 12 minutes.
Ⓐ

7. Remove the baking tray from the oven. Cut the toasts into triangles. Put on individual serving plates.
Ⓐ

Serve hot with tomato ketchup.

JAM PINWHEELS

Makes 6 pinwheels.

What you will need
6   large fresh bread slices
butter
strawberry jam

Equipment needed
butter knife
knife
chopping board
1 serving plate

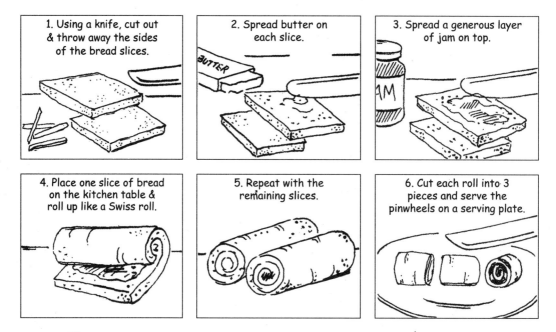

1. Using a knife, cut out & throw away the sides of the bread slices.

2. Spread butter on each slice.

3. Spread a generous layer of jam on top.

4. Place one slice of bread on the kitchen table & roll up like a Swiss roll.

5. Repeat with the remaining slices.

6. Cut each roll into 3 pieces and serve the pinwheels on a serving plate.

You can similarily make Paneer & Chutney Pinwheels.

1.   Noughts and Crosses Pizza, *page 28.*
2.   Strawberry Flip, *page 14.*
3.   Funny Faces, *page 56.*

CHEESE GARLIC BUNS

Makes 6 buns.

What you will need
6   bread buns
4   cloves garlic
½   cup butter
½   cup grated cheese

Equipment needed
grater
knife
cups
mixing bowl
baking tray
oven
1 serving plate

1. Slice each bun horizontally into 2 halves & keep aside.

2. Preheat the oven to 180°C (355°F)

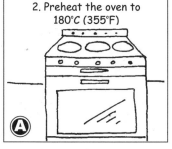

3. Peel & crush the garlic cloves.

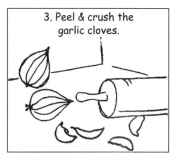

4. Put the butter in a mixing bowl, add the crushed garlic & the cheese & mix well.

5. Spread this mixture on the bun halves & place on a baking tray.

6. Place the baking tray in the preheated oven & bake for 10 to 12 minutes till the cheese melts.

7. Remove the baking tray from the oven.

1. Baked Potatoes, *page 40.*
2. Fresh Fruit Salad, *page 72.*
3. Quick Vegetable Soup, *page 23.*
4. Che-Mato Pasta, *page 38.*

Serve hot.
These taste great with soup.

FUNNY FACES

Makes 4 faces. *Picture on page 53*

What you will need
4 slices bread
½ cup paneer
1 tablespoon mint chutney
1 carrot
1 small capsicum
1 cheese slice
salt to taste

Equipment needed
pastry cutter
peeler
grater
mixing bowl
cup
tablespoon
knife
chopping board
1 serving plate

1. Using a 75 mm. (3") cookie cutter, cut out a circle from each bread slice.

2. Grate the paneer in the mixing bowl & mix with the mint chutney. Add salt if required.

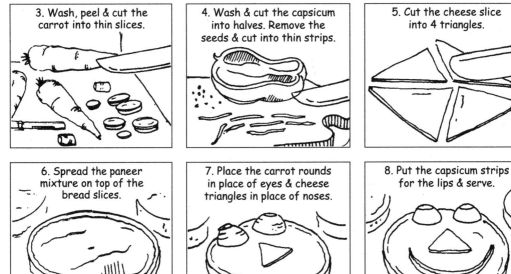

3. Wash, peel & cut the carrot into thin slices.

4. Wash & cut the capsicum into halves. Remove the seeds & cut into thin strips.

5. Cut the cheese slice into 4 triangles.

6. Spread the paneer mixture on top of the bread slices.

7. Place the carrot rounds in place of eyes & cheese triangles in place of noses.

8. Put the capsicum strips for the lips & serve.

Be creative. Use whatever mom has in the fridge to make the faces.

CAKES AND BAKES

BANANA WALNUT MUFFINS

Makes 18 muffins. *Picture on page 35*

What you will need

1 cup butter
1 cup castor sugar
2 bananas
½ cup walnuts, chopped
1 cup plain flour (maida)
½ teaspoon soda bi-carb
½ teaspoon baking powder
½ teaspoon salt
½ teaspoon vanilla essence
3 tablespoons milk
butter to grease the muffin moulds

Equipment needed

sieve
tray
mixing bowl
wooden spoon
knife
teaspoons
tablespoons
oven
18 muffin moulds
1 serving plate

1. Grease the muffin moulds with butter. Keep aside. Preheat the oven to 200°C (400°F)

2. Sieve the flour with the soda bi-carb, baking powder & salt on a tray. Keep aside.

3. Put the butter in a mixing bowl & stir with a wooden spoon till it is soft & creamy.

4. Add the castor sugar slowly, mixing it well.

5. Peel & chop the bananas, add to the butter & sugar mixture & mix well.

6. Add the vanilla essence, the walnuts & sifted flour mixture & mix gently.

7. Add the milk to make a batter-like consistency.

8. Spoon 2 tablespoons of the batter into each greased muffin mould.

9. Place the moulds in the oven & bake for 20 to 25 minutes.

10. Remove from the oven and transfer to a serving plate.

APPLE CINNAMON MUFFINS

Makes 18 muffins. *Picture on page 63*

What you will need

2 apples
1 cup plain flour (maida)
½ teaspoon baking powder
½ teaspoon baking soda
1 cup butter
1 cup castor sugar
1 teaspoon cinnamon powder
½ teaspoon vanilla essence
½ cup walnuts, chopped

2 to 3 tablespoons milk
butter to grease the
muffins moulds

Equipment needed

sieve
knife
chopping board
cups
wooden spoon
teaspoons
tablespoons
mixing bowl
oven
18 muffin moulds
or paper cups

1. Preheat the oven to 200°C (400°F) Grease the muffin moulds & keep aside.

2. Cut the apples into small pieces & keep aside.

3. Sieve the flour with the baking powder & baking soda & keep aside.

4. Put the butter in a mixing bowl & mix with a wooden spoon till soft & creamy.

5. Slowly add the castor sugar, mixing well.

6. Add the apples, cinnamon powder & vanilla essence and mix well.

7. Slowly add in the flour mixture & walnuts.

8. Add 2 to 3 tablespoons of milk & mix gently.

9. Spoon 2 tablespoons of the batter into each muffin mould.

| 10. Place the moulds in the oven and bake for 20 to 25 minutes. | 11. Remove from the oven and transfer to a serving plate. |

Serve warm.

💡 Ask an adult to open the oven and to test whether the muffins are cooked. Insert a wooden toothpick in the centre of the muffins. If the toothpick comes out clean, the muffin is cooked.

CORNFLAKE COOKIES

Makes 15 cookies. *Picture on page 63*

What you will need
½ cup butter
½ cup castor sugar
1 cup plain flour (maida)
½ teaspoon baking powder
1 tablespoon lemon juice
½ teaspoon vanilla essence
1 cup crushed cornflakes

Equipment needed
teaspoon
tablespoons
mixing bowl
wooden spoon
cups
oven
baking tray

| 1. Preheat the oven to 180°C (355°F) | 2. Put the butter in a mixing bowl & using a wooden spoon, beat till it is soft & creamy. | 3. Add the castor sugar & mix well. |

4. Add the flour, baking powder, lemon juice & vanilla essence & mix well using your hands. The mixture should look like a dough.

5. Divide into 15 equal portions & roll in the crushed cornflakes.

6. Place these on a baking tray.

7. Put the tray in the oven & bake for 20 to 25 minutes.

8. Remove the tray from oven.

9. Cool & place the cookies in a cookie jar.

Serve warm or cold.

JAM TARTS

Makes 12 tarts. *Picture on page 35*

What you will need
1   cup plain flour (maida)
½   cup butter
2   tablespoons powdered sugar
¼   teaspoon baking powder
1   to 2 tablespoons cold water
6 tablespoons jam

Equipment needed
mixing bowl   knife
wooden spoon   baking tray
cups   oven
teaspoon   12 small tart moulds
tablespoons   1 serving plate
rolling pin

1. Preheat the oven to 200°C (400°F)

2. Put the butter in a mixing bowl & beat with a wooden spoon till it is soft & creamy. Add the sugar & mix well.

3. Add the flour & baking powder to the butter & sugar mixture & mix well.

4. Slowly add 1 to 2 tablespoons of cold water & gently knead the dough with your hands till it is smooth.

5. Divide the dough into 14 equal rounds.

6. Press 12 rounds into 12 tarts moulds & line the case. Place 1½ teaspoons of jam in each tart.

7. Roll out the remaining 2 rounds into thick puris & cut into thin strips

8. Place two strips in a criss-cross style on each tart. Place the tarts on a baking tray.

9. Bake in the oven for 15-20 minutes. Cool completely, remove from the moulds & transfer to a serving plate.

If you don't have tart moulds, shape the dough into rounds and you have yummy butter cookies.

1. Cornflake Cookies, *page 60*.
2. Chocolate Chip Cookies, *page 67*.
3. Apple Cinnamon Muffins, *page 59*.

CHOCOLATE FUDGE CAKE

Makes 1 cake.

What you will need
For the cake
1 cup plain flour (maida)
¼ cup cocoa powder
¾ cup powdered sugar
½ teaspoon soda bi-carb
½ teaspoon baking powder
6 tablespoons curds
5 tablespoons milk
5 tablespoons melted butter
½ cup chopped walnuts
½ teaspoon vanilla essence
butter to grease the baking tray
walnuts for decoration

For the icing
½ cup icing sugar
4 tablespoons cocoa powder
3 to 4 tablespoons water

Equipment needed
cups
teaspoons
tablespoons
2 mixing bowls
wooden spoon
oven
150 mm. (6") diameter baking tray

1. Preheat the oven to 180°C (355°F)

2. Grease a baking tray with butter. Keep aside.

Recipe continued

1. Submarines, *page 48.*

3. Mix all the cake ingredients in a mixing bowl using a wooden spoon. Make sure there are no lumps.

4. Pour this mixture into the greased baking tray of 150 mm. (6") diameter.

5. Place the tray in the oven and bake for 20 to 25 minutes.

6. Remove the tray from the oven & cool the cake on a wire rack.

7. To make the icing, mix the icing sugar & cocoa powder together & add water to make a thick paste.

8. Pour over the cooled cake. Decorate with walnuts.

Make the icing after the cake has cooled as the icing hardens quickly.

CHOCOLATE CHIP COOKIES

Makes 15 cookies. *Picture on page 63*

What you will need
½ cup butter
1 cup plain flour (maida)
½ cup brown sugar
½ teaspoon vanilla essence
100 grams milk chocolate bar
2 to 3 tablespoons milk

Equipment needed
knife
chopping board
cups
teaspoons
tablespoons
mixing bowl
wooden spoon
baking tray
oven
1 serving plate

1. Preheat the oven to 180°C (355°F).

2. Cut the chocolate bar into small pieces. Keep aside.

3. Put the butter in a mixing bowl & using a wooden spoon, beat till it is soft & creamy.

4. Add the brown sugar & mix well for some time.

5. Add the vanilla essence, flour & chocolate pieces & mix again.

6. Add enough milk to make a dough.

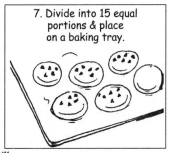

7. Divide into 15 equal portions & place on a baking tray.

8. Put the baking tray in the oven and bake for 30 to 35 minutes.

9. Remove the tray from the oven. Allow to cool & transfer the cookies to a serving plate.

You can roll out the dough using a rolling pin and cut out different shapes for fancy chocolate cookies.

FLAP JACKS

Makes 24 Pieces. *Picture on page 36*

What you will need
1   cup butter
1   cup brown sugar
a pinch of salt
1½ cups quick cooking oats
¼   teaspoon vanilla essence
butter to grease the baking tray

Equipment needed
mixing bowl
wooden spoon
cups
teaspoons
knife
300 mm. x 200 mm. (12"x8") baking tray
oven
1 serving plate

1. Preheat the oven to 200°C (400°F). Grease a baking tray with butter. Keep aside.

2. In a mixing bowl, mix the butter, brown sugar & salt.

3. Using a wooden spoon, mix till the mixture is soft & creamy.

4. Add the vanilla essence & oats & mix well.

5. Spread the mixture onto the greased baking tray using the back of a spoon.

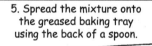

6. Put the tray in the oven & bake for 15-20 minutes.

7. Remove the tray from the oven. It will be soft & bubbling when it is removed.

8. Cool for 10 minutes & cut into 24 pieces using a knife. Leave for 10 more minutes to cool.

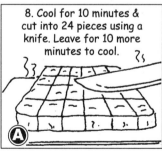

9. Remove from the baking tray & put on a serving plate.

Serve with ice-cream.
Do not touch the mixture when it is removed from the oven because it is very hot.
You can add ½ cup of chopped almond walnuts, peanuts, raisins at step 5 and you have NUTTY FLAPJACKS.

DESSERTS

FUN TRIFLE

Serves 4 to 6.

What you will need
1 sponge cake
3 bananas
1 apple
strawberry jam
fruit juice

For the custard
2½ cups milk
4 tablespoons
custard powder
4 tablespoons sugar

Equipment needed
saucepan
cups
tablespoons
knife
whisk
chopping board
1 glass bowl

1. Mix the custard powder in ½ cup of milk.

2. Boil the rest of the milk with the sugar in a saucepan & add the custard powder mixture.

3. Stir with a whisk till it becomes thick, remove from the fire & allow to cool.

4. Cut the sponge cake horizontally into 2 slices. Apply strawberry jam & sandwich both sides.

5. Cut into 25 mm. (1") pieces.

6. Peel & cut the bananas & apple on a chopping board & keep aside.

7. Arrange one layer of sponge cake pieces on the bottom of a glass bowl.

8. Spread all the fruit on the cake & then pour half the custard on top.

9. Put another layer of sponge cake & top with the remaining custard.

Serve chilled.

Make sure the custard is completely cold before you start making the trifle.

70

BISCUIT CAKE

Makes 1 cake.

What you will need
12 Nice biscuits
1½ cups fresh cream (chilled)
3 tablespoons icing sugar
1 small can (450 grams) pineapple slices
½ cup grated chocolate

Equipment needed
mixing bowl
cups
tablespoons
can opener
grater
whisk
knife
1 serving dish

1. Mix the cream & sugar & whisk till thick. Refrigerate.

2. Open the can of pineapple.

3. Pour the syrup from the can into a bowl.

4. Chop the pineapple into small pieces.

5. Dip 4 biscuits in the pineapple syrup & place on a serving dish to form a rectangle.

6. Spread some cream on it & top with some pineapple pieces.

7. Make 3 more layers in the same way soaking the biscuits well.

8. Top with all the remaining cream.

9. Decorate with grated chocolate.

Chill and serve.

You can also use orange juice and chopped oranges instead of pineapple.
Always store the cake in the refrigerator.

FRESH FRUIT SALAD

Serves 4. *Picture on page 54*

What you will need
2 cups fresh fruits
4 tablespoons sugar
1 cup fresh cream (chilled)
½ teaspoon vanilla essence

Equipment needed
knife
chopping board
cups
teaspoon
tablespoon
2 mixing bowls
whisk
4 serving bowls

1. Cut the fruits into cubes & put in a mixing bowl.

2. Pour the chilled fresh cream into another mixing bowl.

3. Add the sugar & the vanilla essence and whisk till the cream is firm.

4. Divide the fruits equally into 4 serving bowls.

5. Pour the fresh cream over the fruits & serve.

💡 Always store the fresh cream in the refrigerator.
💡 You can use vanilla ice-cream instead of fresh cream.

WALNUT RAISIN TRUFFLES

Makes 20 truffles. *Picture on page 17*

What you will need
1	can (400 grams) condensed milk
3	tablespoons cocoa powder
2	tablespoons butter
1	cup biscuit crumbs
½	cup walnuts, chopped
½	cup raisins

Equipment needed
can opener
rolling pin
saucepan
cups
tablespoons
1 serving plate

1. Open the can of condensed milk.

2. Pour the condensed milk into a saucepan.

3. Add the cocoa powder & butter.

4. Heat the mixture till it boils & keep stirring for about 3 minutes.

5. Remove from the heat & allow it to cool.

6. Add the biscuit crumbs, walnuts and raisins & mix well.

7. Roll the mixture into 20 walnut sized balls & arrange on a serving dish.

8. Refrigerate for an hour.

Serve cold.

To make the biscuit crumbs, put the biscuits in a plastic bag. Seal the top and crush the biscuits with a rolling pin.

FUDGE FINGERS

Makes 20 pieces.

What you will need
2 cups crushed sweet biscuits
1 cup butter
1 cup sugar
2 tablespoons milk
2 tablespoons cocoa powder
½ teaspoon vanilla essence
4 tablespoons chopped walnuts

For the icing
1½ cups icing sugar
2 tablespoons cocoa powder
3 to 4 tablespoons hot water

Equipment needed
saucepan
cups
tablespoons
teaspoon
setting tray
knife
mixing bowl
1 serving tray

1. In a saucepan, mix the butter, sugar, milk & cocoa powder.

2. Heat till all the ingredients melt. Remove from the heat.

3. Add the vanilla essence, walnuts & crushed biscuits and mix well.

4. Pour onto a setting tray & refrigerate for 1 hour.

5. To make the icing, put the icing sugar & cocoa powder in a mixing bowl & add the hot water.

6. Pour this icing over the biscuit mixture.

7. Cut the fudge into 20 pieces.

Served chilled.

Make the icing after the biscuit mixture has set as otherwise it will harden.

JELLY BOATS

Makes 12 boats. *Picture on page 17*

What you will need
½ packet jelly crystals (100 grams)
3 oranges

Equipment needed
knife
saucepan
tablespoon
1 serving plate

1. Cut the oranges into half along with the peel.

2. Carefully remove the orange segments & keep aside.

3. Put the jelly crystals in a saucepan.

4. Add water as specified on the jelly packet.

5. Bring to a boil & cool slightly.

6. Mix well & pour into the orange peel halves.

7. Refrigerate till the jelly sets.

8. Cut each half into 2 segments.

9. Decorate with paper flags to make boats & put on a serving plate.

Chill and serve.

Remove the orange segments carefully using a butter knife.
Use the orange segments to make Fresh Fruit Salad, page 72.

MY FAVORITE RECIPES

No.	Name	Page No.